Mascot Mania

BASKETBALL'S ZANIEST MASCOTS:

FROM BENNY THE BULL TO STUFF THE MAGIC DRAGON

BY DAVID CARSON

Published by Capstone Press, a Capstone imprint.
1710 Roe Crest Drive North Mankato, Minnesota 56003
capstonepub.com

Copyright © 2023 by Capstone. All rights reserved. No part of this publication may be reproduced in whole or in part, or stored in a retrieval system, or transmitted in any form or by any means, electronic, mechanical, photocopying, recording, or otherwise, without written permission of the publisher.

SPORTS ILLUSTRATED KIDS is a trademark of ABG-SI LLC. Used with permission.

Library of Congress Cataloging-in-Publication Data
Names: Carson, David, 1973- author.
Title: Basketball's zaniest mascots : from Benny Bull to Stuff the Magic Dragon / by David Carson.
Description: North Mankato, Minnesota : Capstone Press, 2023. | Series: Mascot mania! | Includes bibliographical references and index. | Audience: Ages 8-11 |
Audience: Grades 4-6 | Summary: "On opening night, a green dragon flies down to the Orlando Magic's court on a zip line. At the Phoenix Suns' arena, a goofy gorilla leaps off a trampoline and slams a big-time dunk. On the Chicago Bulls' court, a fuzzy red bull shoots T-shirts into the crowd. Basketball fans love to laugh and cheer at the shenanigans of these and many other colorful mascots. Have a blast learning about the zaniest basketball mascots!"-- Provided by publisher.
Identifiers: LCCN 2022001274 (print) | LCCN 2022001275 (ebook) | ISBN 9781666347173 (hardcover) | ISBN 9781666353143 (pdf) | ISBN 9781666353167 (kindle edition)
Subjects: LCSH: Basketball--Miscellanea--Juvenile literature. | Sports team mascots--Juvenile literature.
Classification: LCC GV885.1 .C37 2023 (print) | LCC GV885.1 (ebook) | DDC 796.323--dc23/eng/20220604 LC record available at https://lccn.loc.gov/2022001274 LC ebook record available at https://lccn.loc.gov/2022001275

Editorial Credits
Editor: Aaron Sautter; Designer: Terri Poburka; Media Researcher: Morgan Walters; Production Specialist: Polly Fisher

Image Credits
Associated Press: Nick Lisi, spread 20-21; Getty Images: Jamie Squire, spread 12-13, John Biever, spread 28-29, Lance King, spread 14-15, Streeter Lecka, 22; Newscom: Adam Davis/Icon Sportswire ASA, 6, Icon SMI 760/Icon SMI, top right Cover, John Fisher/Cal Sport Media, sread 16-17, MATIAS J. OCNER/TNS, spread 18-19, Stephen M. Dowell/TNS, spread 26-27, Tony Quinn/Icon SMI, 25; Shutterstock: New Africa, 5, Oleksii Sidorov, spread 4-5; Sports Illustrated: Al Tielemans, bottom left Cover, David E. Klutho, top left Cover, top middle Cover, middle Cover, spread 8-9, spread 10-11

All internet sites appearing in back matter were available and accurate when this book was sent to press.

Printed in the United States   5391

Table of CONTENTS

Show Time!	4
The Coyote	6
Benny the Bull	8
Go the Gorilla	10
Big Jay and Baby Jay	12
Rameses and RJ	14
Bango	16
Burnie	18
Otto the Orange	20
Stanford Tree	22
G-Wiz	24
Stuff the Magic Dragon	26
Big Red	28
Glossary	30
Read More	31
Internet Sites	31
Index	32
About the Author	32

SHOW TIME!

Super slam dunks. **Trampoline** trick shots. Rockin' music. And lots of dancing with the fans. With nonstop action and endless energy, basketball is the perfect setting for zany mascots.

Mascots have won fans' hearts at basketball arenas across the nation. Some mascots are high-flying **daredevils**. Others just love taking **selfies** with their young fans. Some are wacky or just plain weird. But no matter what, mascots play a big role in getting fans pumped up during games.

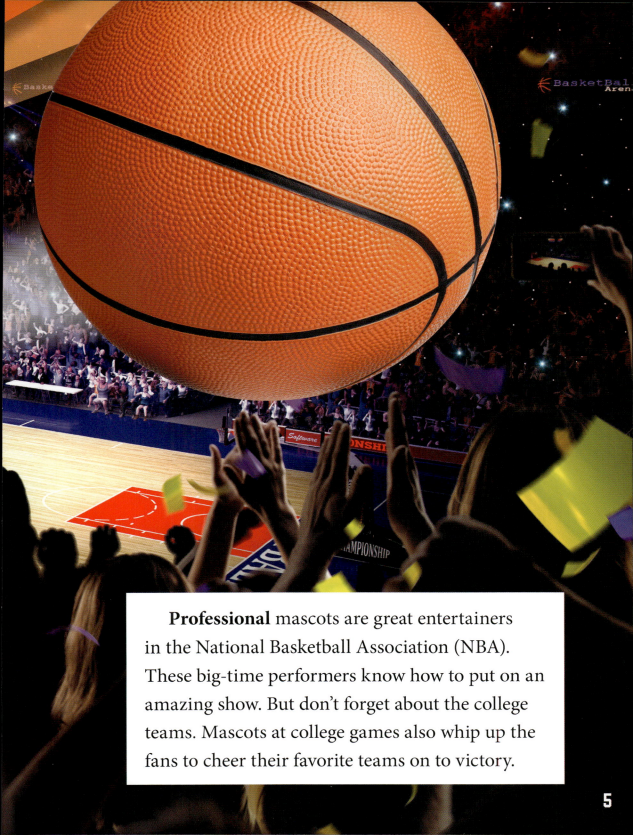

Professional mascots are great entertainers in the National Basketball Association (NBA). These big-time performers know how to put on an amazing show. But don't forget about the college teams. Mascots at college games also whip up the fans to cheer their favorite teams on to victory.

THE COYOTE

Deep in the heart of Texas there's a crazy coyote with big, kooky eyes. He's the mascot for the NBA's San Antonio Spurs. The Coyote loves riding his over-sized tricycle around the court, waving at fans and pumping them up for the game.

The Coyote first joined the Spurs in 1983. He's been a fan favorite ever since. In 2007, the Coyote was inducted into the Mascot Hall of Fame.

The Coyote is part of the Spurs' cowboy **theme**. Many mascots around the country have a t-shirt gun. Fans love it when mascots blast t-shirts into the stands. But a simple t-shirt gun isn't enough for the Coyote. He uses a t-shirt cannon! It can shoot several t-shirts at once high into the seats.

THE MASCOT HALL OF FAME

Halls of fame honor the best of the best in all the major sports. Being in the hall is a huge honor. The Mascot Hall of Fame in Whiting, Indiana, features the most popular mascots from both pro and college sports teams.

★ STATS ★

NAME:
The Coyote

HOME TEAM:
San Antonio Spurs

FIRST APPEARANCE:
1983

FUN FACT:
The Coyote's favorite meal is roadrunner tacos.

BENNY THE BULL

Benny the Bull is the oldest mascot in the NBA. He first appeared as the Chicago Bulls' mascot way back in 1969. He's hard to miss with his bright red hair and an adorable smile.

At first, Benny was pretty mellow. High-fiving and dancing with fans was the norm. But when superstar Michael "Air" Jordan arrived, he quickly became the most exciting player in the NBA. Benny followed Jordan's lead. He soon became the NBA's most exciting mascot.

Benny could probably play in the NBA himself. He's most famous for his thunderous dunks. On the court, Benny springs off a trampoline to do backflips, reverse dunks, and windmills. Benny even jumps through hoops of fire! It's all part of the show for Benny the Bull.

★ STATS ★

NAME:
Benny the Bull

HOME TEAM:
Chicago Bulls

FIRST APPEARANCE:
1969

FUN FACT:
Benny the Bull was the first mascot for an NBA team.

GO THE GORILLA

Go the Gorilla might be one of the most famous mascots in all of sports. But why do the Phoenix Suns have a gorilla for a mascot? It all happened by chance. In the late 1970s, a diehard Suns fan started coming to games dressed in a gorilla costume. The fans loved it. It wasn't long before the team **adopted** Go as the official mascot.

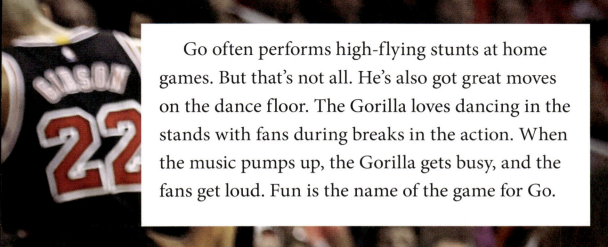

Go often performs high-flying stunts at home games. But that's not all. He's also got great moves on the dance floor. The Gorilla loves dancing in the stands with fans during breaks in the action. When the music pumps up, the Gorilla gets busy, and the fans get loud. Fun is the name of the game for Go.

Did You Know?

Go sometimes rides a custom-built motorcycle onto the court to rev up the crowd at Suns games.

★ STATS ★

NAME:
Go the Gorilla

HOME TEAM:
Phoenix Suns

FIRST APPEARANCE:
1980

FUN FACT:
The Gorilla was inducted into the Mascot Hall of Fame in 2005.

BIG JAY AND BABY JAY

Some college basketball teams also have fun and loveable mascots. Two of the most popular are at the University of Kansas. Big Jay and Baby Jay are over-sized colorful birds. They often steal the show during game time.

The University of Kansas basketball team is nicknamed the "Jayhawks." Big Jay and Baby Jay are named after the **mythical** bird. Big Jay first hatched in 1953. Baby Jay came along in 1971. Big Jay loves to dance with the team's cheerleaders. Meanwhile, Baby Jay helps entertain the youngest fans at Jayhawks games.

BIRTH OF BASKETBALL

The game of basketball was invented by Dr. James Naismith in 1891 at Springfield College in Massachusetts. He later worked at the University of Kansas and coached the school's first basketball team in 1899. More than 120 years later, basketball has become one of the most popular sports in the world.

★ STATS ★

NAME:
Big Jay and Baby Jay

HOME TEAM:
University of Kansas

FIRST APPEARANCE:
1953 (Big Jay), 1971 (Baby Jay)

FUN FACT:
The team's name comes from the nickname "jayhawkers." These were people who fought against slavery both before and during the Civil War.

RAMESES AND RJ

The Dean Smith Center is one of the loudest arenas in the country. It's home to the University of North Carolina Tar Heels basketball team. Tar Heels fans take their basketball very seriously. Leading the charge is Rameses, the Tar Heels' mascot.

Rameses is a tough ram. He doesn't back down from any challenge. He's ready to battle **rivals** like the Duke Blue Devils or North Carolina State Wolfpack.

Rameses first came on the scene in 1987. He's gone through a lot of changes since then. Rameses' little brother, RJ, came along in 2015. RJ is a smaller, friendlier version of Rameses. But he's just as excited for Tar Heel basketball. RJ loves helping his brother rev up the crowd on gameday.

Did You Know?

The name "Tar Heel" dates back to the Civil War. A tar heel was someone who produced tar from pine trees. The tar was used to seal boats and make them waterproof.

★ STATS ★

NAME:
Rameses and RJ

HOME TEAM:
University of North Carolina Tar Heels

FIRST APPEARANCE:
Rameses in 1987; RJ in 2015

FUN FACT:
A real sheep, or ram, named Rameses has been the mascot for the North Carolina football team since 1924.

BANGO

The Milwaukee Bucks have a team saying: "Fear the Deer." But there's no need to be afraid of Bango. When it's time to play ball, the Bucks' mascot is all about fun.

Did You Know?

The famous Harley-Davidson motorcycles are made in Milwaukee, Wisconsin. No wonder Bango loves his "Harley" cruiser!

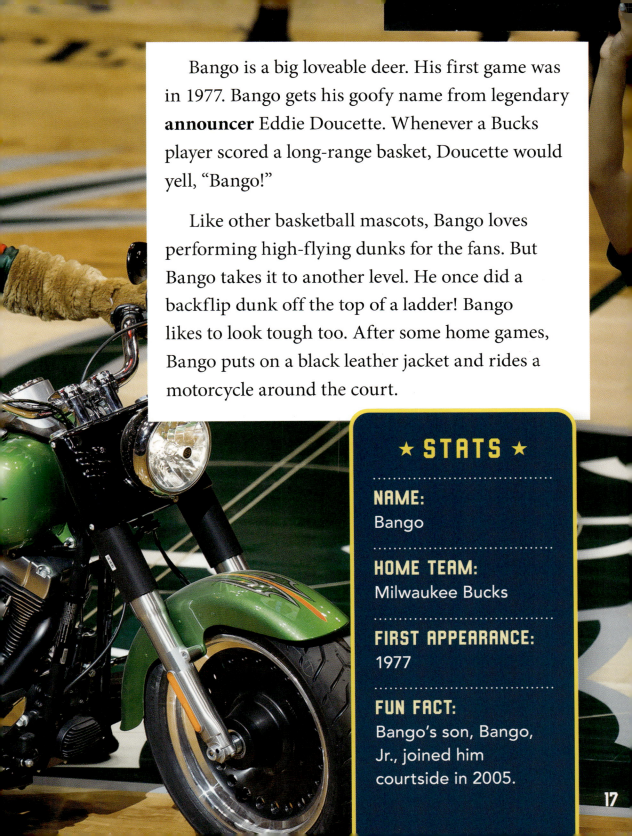

Bango is a big loveable deer. His first game was in 1977. Bango gets his goofy name from legendary **announcer** Eddie Doucette. Whenever a Bucks player scored a long-range basket, Doucette would yell, "Bango!"

Like other basketball mascots, Bango loves performing high-flying dunks for the fans. But Bango takes it to another level. He once did a backflip dunk off the top of a ladder! Bango likes to look tough too. After some home games, Bango puts on a black leather jacket and rides a motorcycle around the court.

★ STATS ★

NAME:
Bango

HOME TEAM:
Milwaukee Bucks

FIRST APPEARANCE:
1977

FUN FACT:
Bango's son, Bango, Jr., joined him courtside in 2005.

BURNIE

Basketball has some really wacky mascots. One of the wackiest roams the court for the Miami Heat in South Florida. Burnie is a big cuddly fireball on two legs. He has flame-red fur and a giant green basketball for a nose.

Burnie could probably suit up for the Heat too. He stands 7 feet, 6 inches (229 centimeters) tall with his spiky hairdo. That would make Burnie one of the tallest NBA players of all time!

★ STATS ★

NAME:
Burnie

HOME TEAM:
Miami Heat

FIRST APPEARANCE:
1988

FUN FACT:
Burnie's favorite food: a peanut butter and spam sandwich. Yum?

Basketball isn't Burnie's only passion. He often makes appearances throughout the Miami community. Burnie makes time to visit schools and birthday parties to meet his young fans. He especially loves visiting hospitals along with the Heat players.

OTTO THE ORANGE

Who, or what, is this? Is it a basketball? Nope. It's a giant orange! One of the oddest oddballs in all of sports is Otto the Orange. This strange fruit is the mascot for Syracuse University. The school's sports teams are nicknamed the "Orange." So what else should their mascot be but an over-sized orange!

Otto first appeared at Syracuse basketball games in the 1980s. Fans quickly fell in love with the jolly fruit on two legs. By 1995 Otto became the school's official mascot. With a button-shaped nose and a huge smile, Otto has entertained fans courtside ever since. He doesn't perform high-flying stunts like other mascots. But what do you expect from a giant fruit?

★ STATS ★

NAME:
Otto the Orange

HOME TEAM:
Syracuse University

FIRST APPEARANCE:
1980s

FUN FACT:
He may be an over-sized fruit, but Otto has his own Instagram and Twitter pages.

The Stanford Tree is another basketball oddity. It isn't the official mascot for Stanford University. Rather, this funny fir tree is the mascot for the Stanford Band.

The Tree first sprouted up in the 1970s. It quickly became a favorite with the Stanford students. By the 1980s, the Tree was appearing at Stanford basketball and football games.

The Tree often appears in different forms. Sometimes it looks like a walking Christmas tree with floppy leaves and a giant toothy smile. Other times it might wear a top hat and have a mustache and giant googly eyes. No matter what shape it takes, the fans love the Tree as one of the wackiest mascots in sports.

Did You Know?

Stanford's team name is "The Cardinal." This refers to the color red, not the songbird.

★ STATS ★

NAME:
The Stanford Tree

HOME TEAM:
Stanford University

FIRST APPEARANCE:
1975

FUN FACT:
The big Tree is a nod to the famous giant redwood trees found near the Stanford campus.

G-WIZ

He's no Harry Potter. He's G-Wiz, the magical mascot for the Washington Wizards. G-Wiz didn't attend Hogwarts. But he's still got a few tricks up his sleeve.

G-Wiz works his magic on the basketball court. He's the biggest trickster in the NBA, and he's entertained Wizards fans since 1997. With a big silly nose and an over-sized wizard hat, G-Wiz is a real goofball. He looks like a cross between Big Bird, Cookie Monster, and a Smurf.

This zany mascot is active off the court too. He loves meeting fans of all ages at schools and marches in parades around Washington, D.C.

★ STATS ★

NAME:
G-Wiz

HOME TEAM:
Washington Wizards

FIRST APPEARANCE:
1997

FUN FACT:
G-Wiz's favorite movie? *The Wizard of Oz* of course!

Did You Know?

G-Wiz isn't the only Wizards mascot. G-Man is a muscle-bound mascot who specializes in daredevil dunks.

The Orlando Magic have their own magical mascot. Stuff the Magic Dragon has entertained Magic fans since the team first joined the NBA.

Stuff hatched from an egg in 1989. Now full grown, he's got spiky pink hair and green fur. Stuff is hard to miss on the court. But this dragon doesn't breathe fire. Instead, he's got colorful party horns that blast from his **snout** when he's excited.

Stuff doesn't look like a typical high-flying stunt mascot. But he loves to put on a show with his monster dunks. He's also a great break dancer. He's known to climb into the stands and get down to some rockin' music with the fans.

★ STATS ★

NAME:
Stuff the Magic Dragon

HOME TEAM:
Orlando Magic

FIRST APPEARANCE:
1989

FUN FACT:
Stuff's best trick is a backflip dunk off the top of a ladder.

Did You Know?

Stuff's name is a reference to *Puff the Magic Dragon*. It was a popular children's cartoon in the 1970s.

BIG RED

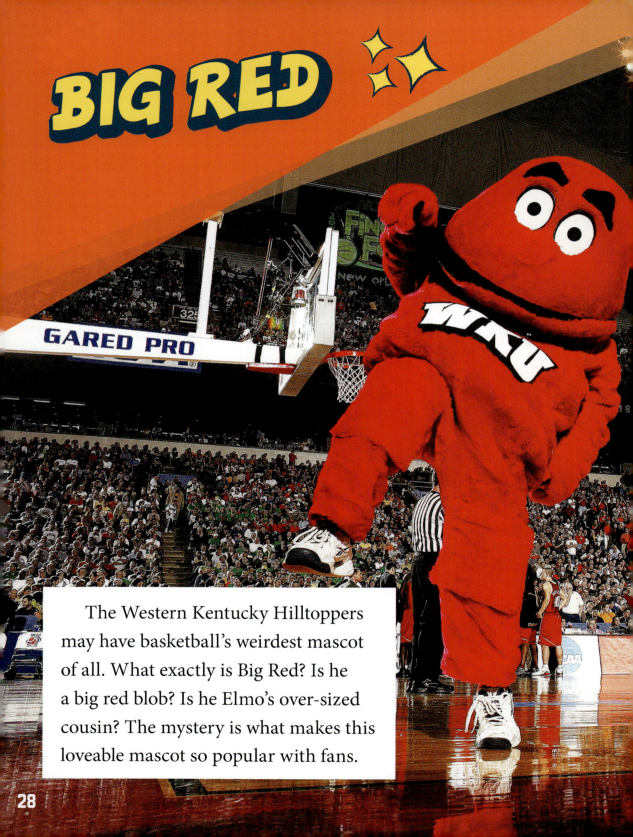

The Western Kentucky Hilltoppers may have basketball's weirdest mascot of all. What exactly is Big Red? Is he a big red blob? Is he Elmo's over-sized cousin? The mystery is what makes this loveable mascot so popular with fans.

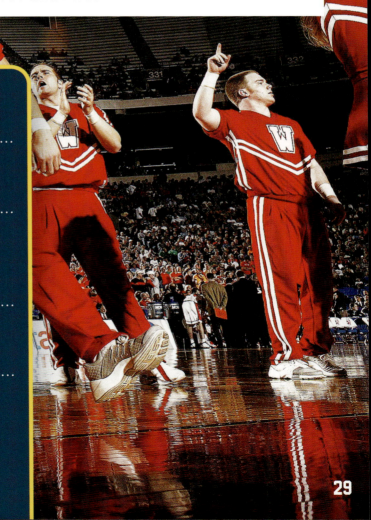

Big Red has a huge grin from ear to ear (if he had ears). Big googly eyes and oversized eyebrows fill out the rest of his face. His look is complete with big "WKU" letters written across his big belly.

Big Red first appeared in 1979 and quickly became a fan favorite. With his huge smile, Big Red is always ready to snap some selfies with the fans. Nobody really knows what this goofy mascot is. He's just Big . . . and Red.

★ STATS ★

NAME:
Big Red

HOME TEAM:
Western Kentucky University

FIRST APPEARANCE:
1979

FUN FACT:
Big Red doesn't talk or make any other noises. He just loves to smile!

GLOSSARY

adopted (uh-DOP-tuhd)—officially accepted and made a part of something

announcer (uh-NAUN-suhr)—a person who describes the action during a sports event

daredevil (DAIR-dev-uhl)—a person who is bold and often takes risks

mythical (MITH-ih-kuhl)—imaginary or not real

professional (pruh-FESH-uh-nuhl)—a person who is paid to do a certain activity

rival (RYE-vuhl)—a person or team that you or your team often compete against

selfie (SEL-fee)—a photograph that is taken by the person who appears in it, usually with a smartphone or other digital camera

snout (SNOUT)—the long, front part of an animal's head

theme (THEEM)—a central idea on which a team bases its colors, logos, and other characteristics

trampoline (TRAM-puh-leen)—a piece of canvas stretched tightly and attached to a frame with elastic ropes or springs

READ MORE

Berglund, Bruce R. *Basketball GOATS: The Greatest Athletes of All Time.* North Mankato, MN: Capstone Press, 2022.

Kelley, KC. *Basketball: Score with STEM!* Minneapolis, MN: Bearport Publishing Company, 2022.

Pryor, Shawn. *Basketball's Most Ridonkulous Dunks!* North Mankato, MN: Capstone Press, 2021.

INTERNET SITES

Junior NBA
jr.nba.com/

Mascot Hall of Fame
mascothalloffame.com

National Collegiate Athletic Association (NCAA)
www.ncaa.com/sports/basketball-men/d1

INDEX

appearance, 6, 8, 12, 17, 18, 21, 23, 24, 25, 27, 29

Chicago Bulls, 8, 9
Civil War, 13, 15

Doucette, Eddie, 17

entertaining fans, 5
   birthday parties, 19
   cheering on teams, 5
   dancing, 4, 8, 11, 12, 27
   high-fives, 8
   parades, 24
   party horns, 27
   riding vehicles, 6, 11, 16, 17
   selfies, 4, 29
   slam dunks, 4, 8, 17, 27
   social media, 21
   stunts, 11, 21, 27
   t-shirts, 7
   trick shots, 4, 8, 17, 25
   visiting schools and hospitals, 19, 24

G-Man, 25

Jordan, Michael, 8

live animal mascots, 15

Mascot Hall of Fame, 7, 11
Miami Heat, 18
Milwaukee Bucks, 16–17

Naismith, James, 13
nicknames, 12, 13, 15, 17, 21, 23, 27

Orlando Magic, 27

Phoenix Suns, 10, 11

San Antonio Spurs, 6–7
Springfield College, 13
Stanford University, 23
Syracuse University, 21

University of Kansas, 12, 13
University of North Carolina, 14, 15

Washington Wizards, 24, 25
Western Kentucky University, 28, 29

ABOUT THE AUTHOR

David Carson is a photographer and freelance writer. He's been a sports fan all his life and loves to root on his favorite NBA team, the Chicago Bulls.